GW00367566

Practice

Comprehension

Brenda Stones

**Age 9–11
Years 5–6**
Key Stage 2

Advice for parents

We are surrounded by things to read: billboards, adverts, circulars, websites, newspapers and, finally, books. The skill we need to develop is how to be a critical reader: to think about where all this stuff is coming from, who wrote it and why, and which pieces we should respond to and how.

This book presents a range of the real kinds of reading that we encounter, and helps children start to sift and sort, skim and scan, so that they develop a better understanding of how to read.

The page of questions that follows each text is similar in style to the National Tests (the SATs):

- Multiple choice question 1, for the child to select a quick answer.
- Short answer questions 2–4, for short phrases of answers.
- Long answer questions 5–6, for more reflectively written sentences.

- Final question 7, often about the child's personal response to the text.
- The '**How have I done?**' section invites your child to revisit the texts and to summarise their findings.
- The '**Teacher's tips**' are written by practising classroom teachers. They give useful advice on specific topics or skills to deepen your child's understanding and confidence and to help you help your child.
- Finally, the answers section gives guidance on how to be a critical reader of each of the texts in the book.

The key difference to the National Tests is that in this book we're not looking for right answers: this is a practice book, not a test book, so we're prompting children to ask the right questions, to learn the process of reading, rather than come up with predicted answers that can be marked.

Every effort has been made to trace all copyright holders, but if any have been inadvertently overlooked the Publishers will be pleased to make the necessary arrangements at the first opportunity.

Although every effort has been made to ensure that website addresses are correct at time of going to press, Hodder Education cannot be held responsible for the content of any website mentioned in this book. It is sometimes possible to find a relocated web page by typing in the address of the home page for a website in the URL window of your browser.

Hachette UK's policy is to use papers that are natural, renewable and recyclable products and made from wood grown in sustainable forests. The logging and manufacturing processes are expected to conform to the environmental regulations of the country of origin.

Orders: you can order online or find your local WHSmith store at: www.whsmith.co.uk.

© Brenda Stones 2013
First published in 2007 exclusively for WHSmith by
Hodder Education
An Hachette UK Company
338 Euston Road
London NW1 3BH

This second edition first published in 2013 exclusively for WHSmith by Hodder Education. Updated, 2014, to reflect National Curriculum changes.
Teacher's tips © Najoud Ensaff 2013

Impression number   10 9 8 7 6 5 4 3
Year   2018 2017 2016 2015 2014

Cover illustration by Oxford Designers and Illustrators Ltd
Character illustrations by Beehive Illustration
All other illustrations by Fakenham Prepress Solutions, Fakenham, Norfolk NR21 8NN
Typeset in 16pt Folio by Fakenham Prepress Solutions, Fakenham, Norfolk NR21 8NN
Printed in Italy

A catalogue record for this title is available from the British Library.

ISBN: 978 1444 188 448

Contents

Welcome to Kids Club! 4

1   Fun poem 6

2   Poem to compare 8

3   Riddle 10

4   Letter 12

5   Playscript 14

6   History textbook 16

7   Historical novel 18

8   Classic verse 20

9   Fantasy novel 22

10   Discussion 24

11   Autobiography 26

12   Persuasion 28

13   Explanation 30

14   Report 32

15   Instructions 34

16   Questionnaire 36

17   Leaflet 38

18   Flier 40

How have I done? 42

Answers 44

Acknowledgements 47

Welcome to Kids Club!

Hi, readers. My name's Charlie and I run Kids Club with my friend Abbie. Kids Club is an after-school club which is very similar to one somewhere near you.

We'd love you to come and join our club and see what we get up to!

I'm Abbie. Let's meet the kids who will work with you on the activities in this book.

My name's Jamelia. I look forward to Kids Club every day. The sports and games are my favourites, especially on Kids Camp in the school holidays.

Hi, I'm Megan. I've made friends with all the kids at Kids Club. I like the outings and trips we go on the best.

Hello, my name's Kim. Kids Club is a great place to chill out after school. My best friend is Alfie – he's a bit naughty but he means well!

I'm Amina. I like to do my homework at Kids Club. Charlie and Abbie are always very helpful. We're like one big happy family.

Greetings, readers, my name's Alfie! Everybody knows me here. Come and join our club; we'll have a wicked time together!

Now you've met us all, tell us something about yourself. All the kids filled in a '**Personal Profile**' when they joined. Here's one for you to complete.

Personal Profile

Name: _____

Age: _____

School: _____

Home town: _____

Best friend: _____

My favourite:

● Book _____,

● Film _____,

● Food _____,

● Sport _____.

My hero is _____ because _____

_____.

When I grow up I want to be a _____.

If I ruled the world the first thing I would do is _____

_____.

If I could be any celebrity for a day, I would be a _____

_____.

INSERT PHOTO OF YOURSELF HERE

This is a poem by Peter Dixon, who has ideas for poems 'anywhere and any time'. This idea came to him while he was filling his car with petrol.

Lost rainbow

One day
coming home from school
(where else?)
I found a rainbow.
Lost
and sad
and torn
and broken
on a garage forecourt.
I picked it up,
wrapped it in a Wonderloaf wrapper
(which was also lost)
and took it home
where I warmed it
and dried it
in front of my mother's fire.
But it died.

I think it must have been
a very old rainbow.

Let's practise

1 This poem is:

free verse ☐

a limerick ☐

a ballad ☐

2 How does this poem make you feel?

_____

3 What four adjectives does the poet use to describe the rainbow?

_____

4 There are no rhymes, but where can you find similar sounds repeated?

_____

_____

5 What do you think might have caused the rainbow, if it did exist?

_____

6 Do you think this poem is about the poet now, or about his childhood? Why?

_____

_____

7 If you met the poet, what do you think he might be like?

_____

_____

Teacher's tips

If you aren't sure what a limerick or ballad is, look up the definition in a dictionary. Limericks and ballads both have rhyme in them. This might help you to answer question 1.

This is another poem by Peter Dixon. This time he remembers finding pictures in the cracks in the bedroom ceiling, when he went to stay with his cousins.

The cracked ceiling

Do you remember the ceiling
With its candles and carrots and flowers?
How we lay in the bed, not quite sleeping
And told stories for hours and hours?
Do you remember the witch with white fingers,
The king with a crown on his head,
And the monster with plastercrack features
Who scowled and hung over the bed?
We told every stain of that ceiling,
We knew every mark from the rain,
And how the great grey anaconda
Swung down from the picture hook rail.
We spotted the face of the devil,
We searched for the treasure of God,
And found the whole story of Noah –
And dragons . . . and mermaids . . . and frogs.
The biggest of all was of Hitler,
He stretched from the middle of Spain
To the notch on the centre rose plaster
Then round to the smoke from the train.
But the best of the cracks on our ceiling,
The thing that we all really liked,
Were the dreams that we had in our pillows
. . . After Billy had switched out the light.

Let's practise

1 Compared with the poem in Unit 1, this is:

same author, different subject ⬭

different author, same subject ⬭

2 Is there any similarity in subject to the poem in Unit 1?

_____

3 What's different about the line lengths and the rhythm?

_____

4 What's different about the rhymes?

_____

5 What was good about lying awake and finding the pictures?

_____

6 Which was the scariest picture? Why?

_____

_____

7 What is the poet's conclusion to the poem?

_____

_____

Teacher's tips

If you get stuck with question 5, have a look at line 4. Think about what the poet did while he lay awake. For question 7, re-read the last few lines – these show you how the poet has ended/concluded his poem.

This is a poem by Leo Aylen, who reads his poetry to audiences in schools. The picture gives you all the clues you need.

RIDDLE

He pressed on the end of the rocket casing.
A soft pink worm
Peeped its head to the light,
Then stretched asleep on top of the forest
Attached to his crowbar.
His face appeared in the window.
Beneath it he opened
The gleaming sluice of the dam, and the river gushed out.
Gently he led both worm and forest
Down to the water to drink and bathe.
Then, lifting his crowbar,
He shoved it into his mouth,
And crushed the body of the worm to bubbles.

1 Which room is this happening in?

Kitchen ☐   Bathroom ☐

Bedroom ☐

2 What is the 'rocket casing'?

_____

3 What is the 'soft pink worm'?

_____

4 What are the 'forest' and 'crowbar'?

_____

5 What is the 'river'?

_____

6 What is he doing?

_____

7 Do you remember if this kind of language is called **simile** or **metaphor**?

Look up both words, and decide which this is.

_____

_____

Teacher's tips

This is a clever poem because it is about a very simple, everyday activity which the poet describes in an imaginative way. Remember to look at the picture to help if you are unsure what the poem is about.

This is a letter from 1783 by the great writer Dr Samuel Johnson, saying what he thought of a poem he'd just read. It is included here partly to set the scene for the playscript that follows.

830. To Sir Joshua Reynolds

Sir   March 4, 1783.

I have sent you back Mr. Crabbe's poem, which I read with great delight. It is original, vigorous, and elegant.

The alterations which I have made I do not require him to adopt, for my lines are, perhaps, not often better than his own; but he may take mine and his own together, and perhaps between them produce something better than either. He is not to think his copy wantonly defaced; a wet sponge will wash all the red lines away, and leave the pages clean.

His Dedication will be least liked: it were better to contract it into a short sprightly address. I do not doubt of Mr. Crabbe's success.

I am, Sir,

Your most humble servant,

Sam: Johnson.

Let's practise

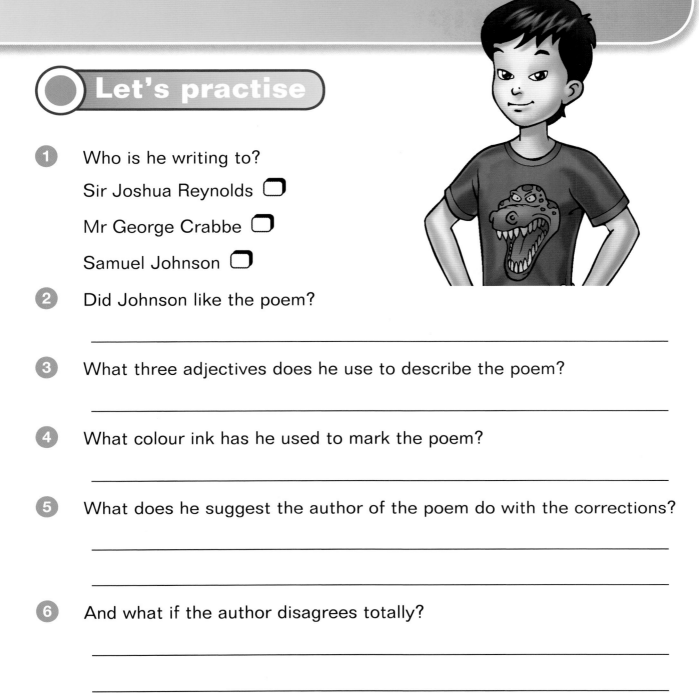

1 Who is he writing to?

Sir Joshua Reynolds ☐

Mr George Crabbe ☐

Samuel Johnson ☐

2 Did Johnson like the poem?

_____

3 What three adjectives does he use to describe the poem?

_____

4 What colour ink has he used to mark the poem?

_____

5 What does he suggest the author of the poem do with the corrections?

_____

_____

6 And what if the author disagrees totally?

_____

_____

7 Which part does Johnson like least?

_____

_____

Teacher's tips

Remember, an adjective is a describing word. Question 5 and question 6 may be tricky. Remember the word _alteration_ can also mean _correction_. This will help you with question 5. For question 6, have a careful look at the last sentence in paragraph 2.

5: Playscript

This is a scene from a modern playscript about the writer Dr Samuel Johnson and his black servant Frank. It was written for radio in 1982 by John Wain.

19. FRANK'S *hurrying feet come down the stairs.*

FRANK: Betsy! Betsy!

BETSY: I'm here, just where I was half an hour ago, mending the same shirt. You don't have to shout the place down.

FRANK: Yes, I do. I have to shout all over this house and all over London and all over the world. Everybody's going to hear what I've got to shout, yes, and the birds up in the sky and the fishes down in the sea.

BETSY: Can I hear what it is, or would that be too much?

FRANK: We're saved, Betsy. Everything's going to be all right. You needn't take in washing, I needn't knock on doors looking for a new job, the children'll have good food and good clothes.

BETSY: Why . . . What miracle has happened?

FRANK: The Doctor's made his will. He's had it witnessed by Mr Strahan and Mr Desmoulins. And guess who it's in favour of.

BETSY: Well, tell me, tell me, put it into words for me!

FRANK: 'My money and property, together with my books, plate and household furniture, to be applied, after paying my debts, to the use of Francis Barber . . . my man-servant, . . . a negro . . .' [*He weeps.*]

1. How many characters are there in this scene?

   One ☐   Two ☐   Three ☐

2. Is Frank's family hard up at the moment? How can you tell?

   _____

   _____

3. What has happened to Dr Johnson?

   _____

4. Which words are quoted from the actual will?

   _____

   _____

5. What does Frank receive as well as money?

   _____

6. What are the only stage directions given?

   _____

   _____

7. What sound effects might you add, as this is radio?

   _____

   _____

Teacher's tips

Remember that for actual words spoken or quotes from a text, speech marks will be used. Look out for these to help you with question 4.

This textbook supplies a fuller recount of Frank Barber's life. It was written by two teachers at Tulse Hill School, in South London.

2 Francis Barber

Francis Barber (Fig. 2.1) was born in Jamaica and was brought to England in 1750 by a Captain Bathurst. Francis was sent to school at Barton in Yorkshire. Capt. Bathurst died in 1752 and gave Francis his freedom.

Francis then became a servant to Dr. Samuel Johnson, a friend of the Bathurst family. Dr. Johnson is most famous as the man who made the first English dictionary. Dr. Johnson sent Francis to school at Bishops Stortford, Hertfordshire. Francis Barber lived with him at his house off Fleet Street, and also at Streatham Place in South London, for many years.

When Dr. Johnson died in 1782 Francis was left his property, an income of £70 a year and all his books and personal possessions. Francis then moved to Lichfield with his wife, Elizabeth, whom he had married in 1776. They ran a school at Burntwood, near Lichfield, until Francis became ill. He died in January 1801 at Stafford Infirmary. Elizabeth Barber carried on teaching for another fifteen years.

Elizabeth and Francis Barber had four children. One of them, Samuel, was a Methodist minister and one grandson emigrated to the United States. Another continued to live in the Staffordshire area.

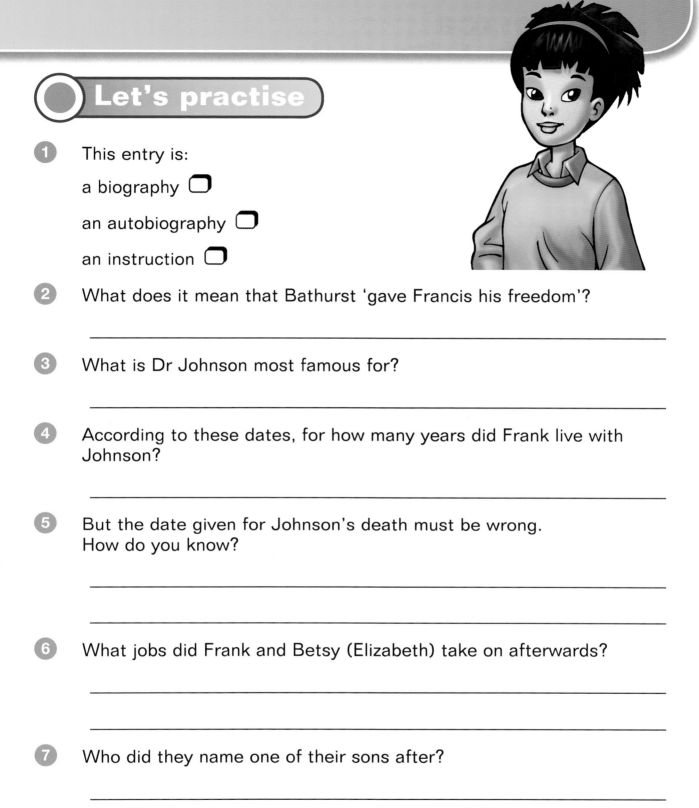

Let's practise

1 This entry is:

a biography ▢

an autobiography ▢

an instruction ▢

2 What does it mean that Bathurst 'gave Francis his freedom'?

_____

3 What is Dr Johnson most famous for?

_____

4 According to these dates, for how many years did Frank live with Johnson?

_____

5 But the date given for Johnson's death must be wrong. How do you know?

_____

_____

6 What jobs did Frank and Betsy (Elizabeth) take on afterwards?

_____

_____

7 Who did they name one of their sons after?

_____

Teacher's tips

For question 2, think carefully about the time when Francis Barber lived and what it was like for black people. For question 5, you will need to think about the other texts you have read. In particular look back at page 12.

7: Historical novel

This is a page from a historical novel based on the true story of Abraham Hannibal, the son of an Ethiopian prince, who was sold into slavery. It was written by Frances Somers Cocks, who travelled to Ethiopia to research the story.

February-April 1704

Chapter 21

SOLD INTO SLAVERY

There followed long months when, time and time again, Abraham nearly did give up hope. There was the slave-market by the Great Mosque at Mecca, where would-be buyers peered at his teeth and his tongue and poked his ribs, and at last a skinny old Turkish merchant called Ahmet bought him and a stock of other slaves and took him away from Tadesse and Afewerk, the last two links with his home. And, as Abraham was led off by his new master, he thought,

I could belong to this man for the rest of my life ... under orders for ever, like a mule or a plough-ox ... That's how he looks at me, as if I was his mule or his ox ...I wonder if Father's slaves felt like this.

168

Let's practise

1 The date when this part of the story happened is:

before the life of Frank Barber ⬭

after the life of Frank Barber ⬭

while Frank Barber was alive ⬭

2 Do you know where the slave-market was?

Ethiopia ⬭   Arabia ⬭   Turkey ⬭

3 What was Abraham feeling when he got to the slave-market?

_____

4 What did they look at, to decide whether to buy Abraham?

_____

5 How did this make Abraham feel?

_____

6 Who do you think Tadesse and Afewerk might be?

_____

_____

7 What is the sign that Abraham was the son of a prince?

_____

_____

8: Classic verse

This is a section from the long poem 'The Pied Piper' by Robert Browning. The real-life story happened in Hamelin in 1284, and Browning published his poem of it in 1849. Read it out loud to hear the rhythm and the rhyme.

Into the street the Piper stept,
Smiling first a little smile,
As if he knew what magic slept
In his quiet pipe the while;
Then, like a musical adept,

To blow the pipe his lips he wrinkled,
And green and blue his sharp eyes twinkled,
Like a candle-flame where salt is sprinkled;
And ere three shrill notes the pipe uttered,
You heard as if an army muttered;

And the muttering grew to a grumbling;
And the grumbling grew to a mighty rumbling;
And out of the houses the rats came tumbling.
Great rats, small rats, lean rats, brawny rats,
Brown rats, black rats, grey rats, tawny rats,

Grave old plodders, gay young friskers,
Fathers, mothers, uncles, cousins,
Cocking tails and pricking whiskers,
Families by tens and dozens,
Brothers, sisters, husbands, wives –
Followed the Piper for their lives.

From street to street he piped advancing,
And step for step they followed dancing,
Until they came to the river Weser
Wherein all plunged and perished!

1. This long poem is a:

   ballad ⬭   riddle ⬭

   haiku ⬭

2. What are the three rhyming verbs in the second verse?

   _____

3. Why do you think the rhythm changes in the third verse?

   _____

   _____

4. Which four adjectives describe the size of the rats?

   _____

5. Which four adjectives describe the colours of the rats?

   _____

6. What job was the piper doing for the town?

   _____

7. Why do you think the last two lines don't fit the rhyme pattern?

   _____

   _____

Teacher's tips

If you are unsure what a ballad, haiku and riddle are, look up the words in a dictionary. The ending is rather sad. Do you think rhyme would have been appropriate? This may help you with question 7.

9: Fantasy novel

This is a page from a modern-day novel called *The Ratastrophe Catastrophe* by David Lee Stone, part of 'The Illmoor Chronicles'. The inspiration for this novel should be obvious.

THE ILLMOOR CHRONICLES

A door burst open somewhere in the southern half of the city. A woman screamed. Nothing happened for a whole minute. Then she was joined by others. Windows were flung open. People rushed out into the streets. A few of the braver citizens were attempting to get a good view of the episode by climbing out on to the rooftops and negotiating precarious slopes filled with damaged slates. Everyone wanted to see what was causing the uproar.

Diek Wustapha was strolling calmly through the streets, a merry melody rising from the flute he raced back and forth between his lips. He had a miniature city-issue map in one hand and stopped at various junctions, regarding it critically.

He was noticed by a couple of citizens on Market Street, not for the fact that he was playing a tune, but because he was seemingly oblivious to the kerfuffle erupting all over the city.

A rat emerged from the open cellar of a tavern in Stainer Street as Bakeman's Brewery Cart unloaded a barrel of ale. It was followed by others, a dozen, a score and a hundred or more. Then a multitude, a million, a mischief.

Let's practise

1. What is the name of the modern Pied Piper?

   _____

2. What do you notice about the length of sentences in the first paragraph?

   _____

   _____

3. What verb is used for how Diek played his flute?

   _____

4. What is the very modern object he is carrying?

   _____

5. What does 'seemingly oblivious to the kerfuffle' mean?

   _____

   _____

6. It's a great last sentence! What do you notice about the author's choice of words?

   _____

7. Does this page make you want to read the whole novel? Why?

   _____

   _____

Teacher's tips

For question 3, it might help you to know that the verb/doing word used is one that suggests speed! If you are unsure what the words *oblivious* and *kerfuffle* mean, remember you can always look them up in a dictionary.

10: Discussion

Here is a magazine article written by the author Terry Deary, who wrote the *Horrible Histories* series. Do you agree with his point of view?

Boys like non-fiction

It's a quirk of nature. It's no use trying to force-feed them fiction. You can tell them what they are 'missing' till you are black and blue in the face (and read all over) but it's like training a cat to sit. Thankless and pointless and against their nature. Yet invariably when the great and the good say, 'Boys don't read - *sigh*!' they mean 'Boys don't read *fiction*.'

Boys' books are under-valued

If boys lean towards non-fiction then what messages do they get from the schools, libraries and book industry? The message is, 'Fiction is superior.' In schools they teach pupils to read using *fiction*. The books they read in class are *fiction*. The writing they are asked to produce is *fiction*. The books that win prizes and get publicity are *fiction*. The great god *fiction*. I've published about sixty fiction and sixty non-fiction books, so I have no personal axe to grind - but I am tired of hearing the non-fiction dismissed as 'text books' that just accumulate facts and don't need a writer's art to create.

Boys know what is good for them

Humans existed on this earth for over a million years without books. They overcame the most incredible hardships to succeed and become the world's top ape. They did it without books. And still, today, most of the greatest icons of success - the sports, television, pop music and film stars - have made it without books. (When did you last hear a footballer say, 'Well, Barry, I owe it all to the inspiration of *The Wind in the Willows*'?) Maybe boys are *right* to reject those overtures to read. Maybe you should get on with your life and turn to books in later years (in my case) or not at all.

1 This point of view was printed in a

newspaper ⬭

magazine ⬭

book ⬭

2 Does the author of this piece write fiction or non-fiction?

_____

3 What are the three groups of people he thinks are pushing for fiction?

_____

4 What are the four ways in which he thinks fiction gets priority?

_____

_____

5 What skill does he think is needed to create non-fiction books?

_____

6 Does he think that celebrities owe their success to reading?

_____

7 Do you agree with the author, or do you think he is being too sweeping about 'all boys'?

_____

_____

Teacher's tips

If you're not sure what the *Horrible Histories* series is, do an internet search to find out. For question 5, look at the last sentence in the second paragraph – this might help you.

11: Autobiography

This is a magazine article by Ian McMillan, who is a writer and poet, and has been Poet in Residence at Barnsley Football Club.

There were things to read in our house for as long as I could remember, but they weren't always books - to start with they were comics. I'm not one of those people who thinks that books are somehow more important than comics, and the recent popularity of graphic novels would seem to bear that out.

My mother used to go to the next village once a fortnight on the bus to get her hair done and on the way back she'd call at the newsagent and bring me a bundle of comics in a brown paper parcel. I can still remember the smell of that parcel and the comics inside: **The Dandy, The Beano, The Victor, The Valiant**. For a short time I got an odd comic called **The Sparky**, and sometimes I got **The Beezer**. When I was very small my favourite character was Rodger the Dodger in (I think) **The Dandy**. He was a kid who was always trying to get out of housework or schoolwork by referring to one of his many books of Dodges. Like lots of other readers I thought that I could live my life like Rodger and I started to make a book of Dodges although I never got further than three or four. I was always trying to do things that kids in comics did and once, after Lord Snooty and His Pals made a lot of money out of painting pebbles yellow and pretending that they'd found gold, I did the same, putting up a notice in the back garden, 'Gold Found on Barnsley Road'. Sadly nobody came to look, not even Mr. Page from next door, who could usually be relied upon to take part in my daft schemes.

Let's practise

1   This piece is:

    discussion ⬭

    biography ⬭

    autobiography ⬭

2   Which comment here agrees with Terry Deary's point of view?

_____

_____

3   Who bought Ian's comics for him?

_____

4   What does he remember about the comics arriving home?

_____

5   What two things did he do as a result of reading *The Dandy*?

_____

_____

6   What lasting skills do you think he gained from reading comics?

_____

_____

7   Do you think he moved on to reading books after reading comics?

_____

Teacher's tips

Remember, a biography is written about someone by someone else but an autobiography is self-written. In case you forgot, Terry Deary wrote the article on page 24. You need to have read this in order to answer question 2.

This is part of a poem that Ian McMillan wrote for the RSPB magazine *Bird Life*, to persuade us to help this seabird.

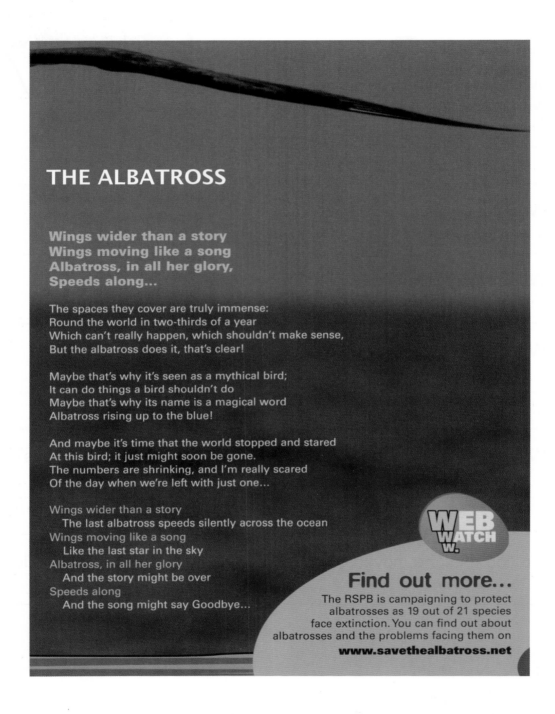

THE ALBATROSS

Wings wider than a story
Wings moving like a song
Albatross, in all her glory,
Speeds along...

The spaces they cover are truly immense:
Round the world in two-thirds of a year
Which can't really happen, which shouldn't make sense,
But the albatross does it, that's clear!

Maybe that's why it's seen as a mythical bird;
It can do things a bird shouldn't do
Maybe that's why its name is a magical word
Albatross rising up to the blue!

And maybe it's time that the world stopped and stared
At this bird; it just might soon be gone.
The numbers are shrinking, and I'm really scared
Of the day when we're left with just one...

Wings wider than a story
    The last albatross speeds silently across the ocean
Wings moving like a song
    Like the last star in the sky
Albatross, in all her glory
    And the story might be over
Speeds along
    And the song might say Goodbye...

WEB WATCH w.

Find out more...
The RSPB is campaigning to protect albatrosses as 19 out of 21 species face extinction. You can find out about albatrosses and the problems facing them on
www.savethealbatross.net

1 What does the RSPB protect?

Birds ⬭   Animals ⬭

Children ⬭

2 Which lines rhyme in each verse?

_____

3 How does the last verse echo the first verse?

_____

_____

4 Which real-life fact does the poet include?

_____

5 What does he mean by the word 'mythical'?

_____

_____

6 Where does the magazine lead us, after the poem?

_____

_____

7 Do you think a poem is a good way of persuading people to take action?

_____

_____

Teacher's tips

If you get stuck on question 4, look carefully at the second verse. For question 6, the bottom right hand corner is a good place to look.

13: Explanation

This is the website we are sent to at the end of the poem in Unit 12. It gives an explanation of the problem that is threatening the albatross.

Save the Albatross

The campaign

The campaign (home)

ALBATROSSES

THE PROBLEM

SOLUTIONS

The problem

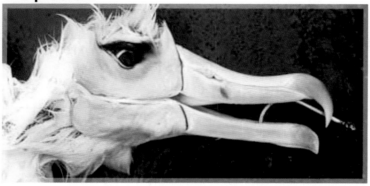

Too many needless and horrid deaths

100,000 albatrosses die each year on fishing hooks. They are being killed in such vast numbers that they can't breed fast enough to keep up. This is putting them in real danger of extinction.

Death on a hook

Picture the scene. One minute you're an albatross gliding across the ocean majestically. You spot a fishing boat, surrounded by other birds, and you know from experience that it offers an easy meal (might be discarded fish waste or bait).

You swoop in to pick up a particularly tasty piece of squid.

As you swallow the bait down, there is a sudden, terrible pain.

The hook embedded in the bait catches and rips your throat. Helplessly, you find yourself dragged down into dark, cold waters.

You choke and drown and are dragged deep down below the surface.

You're unnoticed until your bedraggled corpse is hauled up and discarded.

This happens to an albatross around once every five minutes.

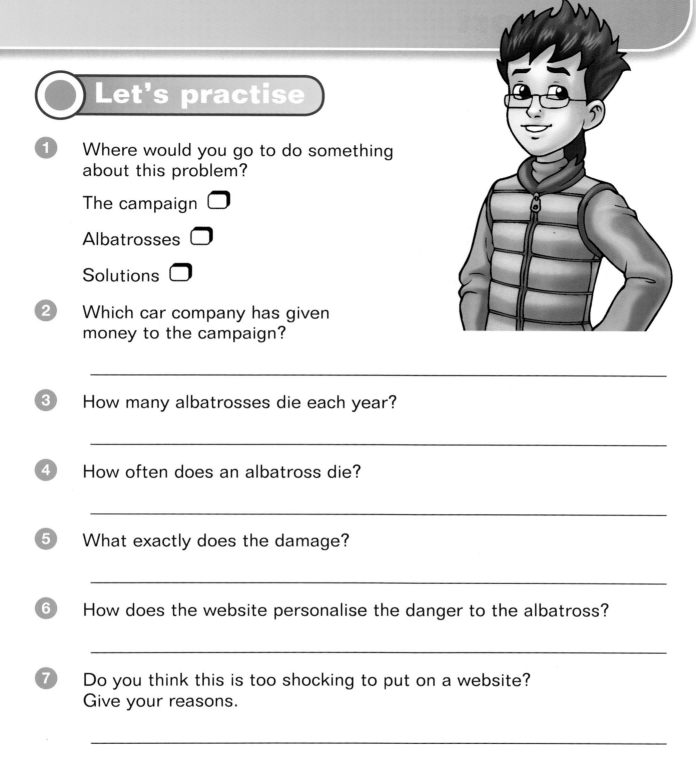

Let's practise

1 Where would you go to do something about this problem?

The campaign ▢

Albatrosses ▢

Solutions ▢

2 Which car company has given money to the campaign?

_____

3 How many albatrosses die each year?

_____

4 How often does an albatross die?

_____

5 What exactly does the damage?

_____

6 How does the website personalise the danger to the albatross?

_____

7 Do you think this is too shocking to put on a website?
Give your reasons.

_____

_____

Teacher's tips

To answer question 1 and question 2, look at the links and images at the top of the website. Remember, a text can be personalised in many ways. Personal pronouns like *we, us,* and *you* as well as images make things personal.

This page from a children's nature magazine offers three sections of information about ladybirds.

It's fun to look out for ladybirds, and because they come in lots of different colours, they can be quite easy to see. The most commonly seen ladybird in the UK is the seven-spot ladybird. There are more than 40 kinds of ladybird altogether, but they're not all brightly coloured and some don't look like the 7-spot ladybird at all!

Like all beetles, ladybirds have two pairs of wings: the back wings are see-through and the front wings are the hard wing cases. Many ladybirds have brightly-coloured wing cases to warn things that might try to eat them that they don't taste nice.

Most ladybirds eat small bugs and aphids (which are also called greenflies). A female adult ladybird can munch more than 60 aphids a day. That adds up to more than 12,000 aphids in her lifetime! Male ladybirds only eat about 30 aphids a day.

Photo by David Norton (rspb-images.com)

Ladybird life cycle

- In spring, ladybirds lay up to 1,000 eggs on plant stems.

- The eggs hatch into grey grub-like creatures called larvae.

- The larvae grow very quickly and literally burst out of their skin three times, which is known as moulting. After that they become pupae. It is at this stage that they undergo dramatic changes and after about a week come out as adult ladybirds. From being eggs to becoming adult ladybirds takes just over a month.

- Nettle patches are good places to look out for ladybirds in spring and early summer (but try not to get stung). Ladybirds only live for about a year and they have to eat as much as possible over the summer months to help them to last through the winter.

Artwork by Chris Shields, Andy Hamilton and Remy Ware

The
ladybird
life cycle

December / January / November / February / October / March / September / April / August / May / July / June

12

1. The ladybird is a kind of:

   beetle ☐

   bird ☐

   spider ☐

2. What is the most common number of spots?

   _____

3. What do the spotted wing cases also serve as?

   _____

4. Who eats more, the male or the female ladybird?

   _____

5. How long does a ladybird live?

   _____

6. Where would you look to find a ladybird?

   _____

7. Which of the three forms of information did you find easiest to read? Why?

   _____

   _____

Teacher's tips

Answers to questions generally appear in order, so the answer to question 1 comes earlier in the text than the answer to question 5. For question 7, look at the paragraphed text, the bullet points and the life cycle diagram. Which do you prefer?

These are rules for using a magnifying glass, as published in a children's nature magazine.

Explore
nature with a...
magnifying glass

Follow these simple rules for using a magnifying glass or hand lens and you will see much more.

If you want to go on a **bug hunt**, get down on your hands and knees first. You won't be able to get a good look at a minibeast through your magnifying glass if you haven't spotted it first.

Move slowly and keep your shadow off your minibeast. Insect eyes can detect movement and your minibeast may hide if it sees you coming.

Whenever possible, **steady the glass** with both hands – you will see much clearer that way.

If you want to see under something but can't look at it directly, slip a **small mirror under it** and then use the **magnifying glass** on the reflection.

If you pick up a creature to have a closer look, try to put it back exactly where you found it. If you find a **minibeast** under a log, **put it back under the same log** – the next log along may look the same to you and me but to an insect, it will be as different as someone else's bedroom.

Protect your lens from scratches – blow any sand or dust off before cleaning it gently with a soft cloth. Magnifying lenses aren't usually as tough as spectacles or binocular lenses.

Never leave your magnifying glass out in the sunshine. The heat from sunlight shining through it could start a fire.

Drawings by Mike Spoor (Bright Agency)

1. These instructions are:

   rules ☐

   directions ☐

   a recipe ☐

2. What symbol is used for the bullet points?

   _____

3. Where should you start reading the rules, and how do you know this?

   _____

   _____

4. List the imperative verbs in the first three rules.

   _____

5. What sentence construction is used at the beginning of three entries, before imperatives?

   _____

6. What subheading could you give to the last two points?

   _____

7. What type styles are used in the main heading, to attract your attention?

   _____

   _____

Teacher's tips

Remember, imperative verbs are instructions or commands such as *get* or *read*.
The last two points are the ones that appear right at the bottom of the page.
For question 7, the 'type styles' are the print used in the heading.

These questions were put to Kate Humble, BBC wildlife presenter with Bill Oddie, in the same children's nature magazine.

Kate with Wildlife Explorer Jenny Daniels

A Wildlife Explorer asks...

Imagine you met a celebrity by accident and you only thought of the questions you would have really liked to have asked them...afterwards. Wildlife Explorer Jenny Daniels was on holiday on the Isle of Mull when she bumped into Kate, who was filming there. Jenny said meeting Kate was the best thing about her trip. We asked Jenny if she had any questions she would like us to put to Kate.

 Do you find the job of being a TV presenter tiring but rewarding?

'Yes I do. It's probably the best job in the world. Sometimes I feel a bit guilty because it seems too much fun to be a proper job. But it does mean I'm away a lot, so I miss friends' birthdays, people's weddings and all that kind of thing.'

 Did you have to have any special qualifications to become a TV presenter?

'I did work in TV production for some years and that was useful in learning about how a programme is made. But the thing you need to have to be a presenter is an inquiring mind. And you must have a passion for finding out things from experts and then telling people about them in a way that makes sense. I get the chance to meet some of the best scientists and ask them anything I like.'

 Do you enjoy travelling from one place to another, or would you prefer to stay in one place for longer?

'I was born with itchy feet and I've always loved travelling. When I was little, I decided that when I grew up I wanted to be in a circus, a gypsy or a Red Indian. They all involve horses and moving around.'

Kate's tip...
for wildlife watching

'When you go out looking for wildlife, you can't go out and say, I'm definitely going to see a water vole, a roe deer, or whatever. Half of the fun is getting to a place you like, sitting down and watching quietly to see what happens. Be a bit patient and wait for the unexpected.'

Let's practise

1 Kate and Jenny met in:

Scotland ⬭

Wales ⬭

Ireland ⬭

2 Did Jenny ask Kate these questions when she met her?

_____

3 What are the downsides to being away so much?

_____

4 What does Kate say are her three skills for the job?

_____

_____

5 What three jobs did Kate dream of when she was a child?

_____

6 What is Kate's tip for getting into the right state of mind for the job?

_____

_____

7 Which is the most 'open-ended' question that Jenny asks?

_____

_____

Teacher's tips

To answer question 1 you will need to find out where the Isle of Mull is. To answer question 7, look carefully at the questions Jenny asks. The ones that provide Kate with possible responses are not open-ended questions.

This is from a leaflet advertising the craft village of Barleylands, in Essex.

Craft Village

THE CRAFT VILLAGE houses probably the largest collection of working crafts in East Anglia.

Visit over **30** impressive, individual, specialist workshops and watch the various artisans at work producing their original and unusual gifts before your very eyes.

Whatever the celebration, you will be sure to find that special gift. You can also arrange an individually commissioned item in many of the workshops.

Come along and our craftsmen and women will be only too happy to help.

RELAX in the beautifully landscaped, paved courtyards and order a cream tea from our tearoom. Light lunches and refreshments are also available all day, with our restaurant serving set lunches and evening meals.

There is easy access to the studios for everyone. The whole village has a paved level surface which enables stress-free wheelchair and pushchair access with the upper level accessed via our lift, if required. Separate disabled parking is also available close by.

Free Entrance - Free Parking!

Craft Village Key to Map

1. Craft Village Entrance from main car park
2. Blacksmiths Forge
3. Craft Village Studio (12)
4. Retail studios (9-11 Upper)
5. Glassblowers Studios and viewing gallery
6. Barleylands Offices
7. Barleylands bus stop
8. Magic Mushroom Restaurant
9. Tea Rooms
10. Toilets and baby changing facilities
11. Craft Village Studios (14 -20 Ground, 21-30 Upper)
12. Craft Village Studios (1-4 Ground, 5-8 Upper)
13. Craft Village Studios (31-37)
14. Pottery Barn
15. Miniature Railway Station

Let's practise

1 From the key to the map, how many studios are there altogether?

30 ◯   36 ◯   37 ◯

2 What does the second paragraph suggest you would want a craft object for?

_____

3 What does the fifth paragraph suggest you do?

_____

4 What is the sixth paragraph about?

_____

_____

5 Why do you think the viewing gallery is above the glassblowers' studios?

_____

_____

6 Give directions to get from the car park to the tea rooms.

_____

_____

7 What would it cost to take in a family of four people?

_____

Teacher's tips

Question 1 might be a bit tricky. Add up the number of studios in the key. You will notice one unlucky number is missing. Question 7 may well be a trick question. Look carefully at the leaflet.

This is a publicity handout for a new play.

Let's practise

1 What is the title of the play?

The Wolves in the Walls ☐

A Musical Pandemonium ☐

National Theatre of Scotland ☐

2 Who wrote the story?

Neil Gaiman and Dave McKean ☐

The National Theatre of Scotland ☐

The Wolves in the Walls ☐

3 What age group is suggested for the audience?

_____

4 Who has already said it's a good play?

_____

5 What does 'Pandemonium' actually mean? Check in your dictionary!

_____

6 Would the illustration make you pick up this flyer? Why?/Why not?

_____

_____

7 Tick which of these adjectives could be used to describe the show:

scary ☐   funny ☐   musical ☐   peaceful ☐   shocking ☐

Teacher's tips

All the information you need is right in front of you. Look carefully at the page after you read each question to spot the answer you're looking for.

How have I done?

1   **Who** were the authors or originators of the texts in this book?

Fill in the names and page numbers in the right columns.

Individual writers	Organisations or companies
p.6 Peter Dixon	

2   **Why** were these texts written?

This time fill in the kinds of text and their page numbers.

For the reader to enjoy and learn	For the reader to take some action
p.6 Fun poem	

3 **Who** is the intended audience?

Mainly children	Mainly adults
p.6 Fun poem	

4 **How** are the texts laid out? Check back to each piece.

Text	Features
p.6 Fun poem	Irregular length of lines, no rhymes
p.8 Poem to compare	
p.10 Riddle	
p.12 Letter	
p.14 Playscript	
p.16 History textbook	
p.18 Historical novel	
p.20 Classic verse	
p.22 Fantasy novel	
p.24 Discussion	
p.26 Autobiography	
p.28 Persuasion	
p.30 Explanation	
p.32 Report	
p.34 Instructions	
p.36 Questionnaire	
p.38 Leaflet	
p.40 Flier	

Teacher's tips

For tables 1–3, look back at each page in the book. Decide which of the two statements at the top of each table describes the passage, poem or advert best. For the last table, put on your thinking cap!

Answers

UNIT 1
1 Free verse
2 It probably makes you feel amused and inspired but slightly sad.
3 Lost, sad, torn, broken
4 wrapped, wrapper; home, warmed; dried it, it died
5 It might have been the kind of rainbow you sometimes see in oil.
6 More likely in his childhood, when he was coming home from school.
7 He sounds gentle and imaginative and funny.

UNIT 2
1 Same author, different subject
2 It's about childhood memories and imagination again.
3 This time the lines are all of similar length, about eight–ten syllables, in a rhythm of triplets.
4 Lines 2 and 4, 6 and 8 etc rhyme, though not always in exact rhymes.
5 The good thing was telling stories for hours and hours.
6 Probably Hitler, because he was the biggest, and maybe this was during or just after the war with Hitler
7 That the best thing after the talking was the dreams they had about the pictures on the ceiling

UNIT 3
1 Bathroom
2 The toothpaste tube
3 The toothpaste
4 The toothbrush
5 The tap water
6 Brushing his teeth
7 It's metaphor, because the poem says the images are the real-life objects.

UNIT 4
1 Sir Joshua Reynolds
2 Yes. He says 'I read with great delight.'
3 original, vigorous, elegant
4 red
5 Combine them with his own alterations
6 Just wash the red lines away with a wet sponge!
7 The Dedication

UNIT 5
1 Two
2 Yes: Betsy has to take in washing, and Frank is looking for a new job.
3 Dr Johnson has died and left a will.
4 The last speech: from 'My money' to the end.
5 House, books, crockery, furniture
6 Frank hurrying down the stairs, and then weeping
7 Frank's feet on the stairs; maybe sounds of the children

UNIT 6
1 A biography
2 Frank must have been a slave in Jamaica.
3 Making the first English dictionary
4 Thirty years
5 The date of the letter on page 12 is 1783. In fact Johnson died in 1784.
6 They became teachers.
7 Samuel Johnson

UNIT 7
1 Before the life of Frank Barber
2 Arabia
3 Nearly giving up hope
4 His teeth, his tongue and his ribs
5 Like the merchant's mule or ox
6 They were other boys from the group of slaves.
7 His own father had also had slaves.

UNIT 8
1 Ballad
2 wrinkled, twinkled, sprinkled
3 To suggest the sound of the coming of the rats
4 Great, small, lean, brawny
5 Brown, black, grey, tawny
6 He was a rat-catcher, or pest controller.
7 They mark an end to the story of the lives of the rats.

UNIT 9
1 Diek Wustapha
2 Short sentences, to build the suspense
3 raced
4 A miniature city-issue map
5 That he appeared to take no notice of the crowd gathering
6 He uses three words beginning with the same letter. This is called alliteration.
7 Any imaginative response

UNIT 10

1. Magazine
2. An equal number of fiction and non-fiction books
3. schools; libraries; the book industry
4. teaching pupils to read; reading in class; pupils' writing; winning prizes and getting publicity
5. A writer's art
6. No, he doesn't think that footballers, for instance, owe their success to reading.
7. Any opinion. Ask 'Why?' to encourage discussion.

UNIT 11

1. Autobiography
2. 'I'm not one of those people who thinks that books are somehow more important than comics.'
3. His mother
4. The brown paper parcel and its smell
5. Make a book of Dodges; paint pebbles yellow to sell as gold
6. Identifying with the characters he read about, making books, living by his imagination
7. Actually he did move on to reading CS Lewis, *Tarzan*, *Billy Bunter*, *Just William*, *Biggles*, and then science fiction.

UNIT 12

1. Birds
2. Lines 1 and 3; 2 and 4
3. It repeats the first verse, with an extra line added after each line of the first verse.
4. An albatross flies round the world in two-thirds of a year.
5. The albatross features in a lot of myths and legends, for example 'The Rime of the Ancient Mariner' by Samuel Taylor Coleridge.
6. To the website for Save the Albatross
7. Encourage discussion.

UNIT 13

1. Solutions
2. Volvo
3. 100,000
4. Every five minutes
5. The hook embedded in the bait
6. It uses the second person, for you the albatross.
7. Yes or no. Encourage discussion.

UNIT 14

1. Beetle
2. Seven
3. Wings
4. The female: twice as much!
5. One year
6. Nettle patches
7. Any opinion, backed up with a reason

UNIT 15

1. Rules
2. A magnifying glass with an eye
3. Top right, because it starts with going on a bug hunt
4. get down, Move, keep, steady
5. If you…
6. Looking after your magnifying glass
7. Four different type sizes, and three different colours of type

UNIT 16

1. Scotland
2. No, she thought of them afterwards.
3. Missing friends' birthdays and weddings
4. having worked in TV production; an inquiring mind; being able to explain things to people
5. circus; gypsy; Red Indian
6. Don't expect to see something definite; just be patient and wait for the unexpected.
7. 'Did you have to have any special qualifications …?'; the other two suggest the answers that Kate might want to give

UNIT 17

1. 36, because there's no number 13
2. As a gift
3. Relax and eat
4. Access for people with disabilities and other special needs
5. It's probably hot with the furnaces, so easier to view from above.
6. Take the second turning right, and it's at the end on your left.
7. Nothing – until you start buying refreshments or gifts!

UNIT 18

1 The Wolves in the Walls
2 Neil Gaiman and Dave McKean
3 Everyone over seven who is not a scaredy cat
4 *The Guardian* and the *Daily Telegraph*
5 Where all the demons live!
6 Yes or no, with plausible reason
7 scary; funny; musical; shocking

How have I done?

1

Individual writers	Organisations or companies
p.6 Peter Dixon	p.30 Save the Albatross website
p.8 Peter Dixon	
p.10 Leo Aylen	p.32 Nature magazine
p.12 Dr Samuel Johnson	p.34 Nature magazine
p.14 John Wain	p.36 Nature magazine
p.16 Textbook authors	p.38 Barleylands
p.18 Frances Somers Cocks	p.40 Theatre
p.20 Robert Browning	
p.22 David Lee Stone	
p.24 Terry Deary	
p.26 Ian McMillan	
p.28 Ian McMillan	

2

You could make a slightly different choice, but this is our suggested answer:

For the reader to enjoy and learn	For the reader to take some action
p.6 Fun poem	p.12 Letter
p.8 Poem to compare	p.24 Discussion
p.10 Riddle	p.28 Persuasion
p.14 Playscript	p.30 Explanation
p.16 History textbook	p.34 Instructions
p.18 Historical novel	p.36 Questionnaire
p.20 Classic verse	p.38 Leaflet
p.22 Fantasy novel	p.40 Flier
p.26 Autobiography	
p.32 Report	

3

You could make a slightly different choice, but this is our suggested answer:

Mainly children	Mainly adults
p.6 Fun poem	p.12 Letter
p.8 Poem to compare	p.14 Playscript
p.10 Riddle	p.24 Discussion
p.16 History textbook	p.26 Autobiography
p.18 Historical novel	p.38 Leaflet
p.20 Classic verse	p.40 Flier
p.22 Fantasy novel	
p.28 Persuasion	
p.30 Explanation	
p.32 Report	
p.34 Instructions	
p.36 Questionnaire	

4

Here are just a few:

Text	Features
p.6 Fun poem	Irregular length of lines, no rhymes
p.8 Poem to compare	More regular length of lines, and rhymes
p.10 Riddle	Short verse with illustration as clue
p.12 Letter	Letter form
p.14 Playscript	Playscript form
p.16 History textbook	Short chapter of text, and illustration
p.18 Historical novel	Chapter opening with date; thoughts in italics
p.20 Classic verse	5 verses with strong rhythm and rhyme
p.22 Fantasy novel	Continuous text
p.24 Discussion	Subheadings to signpost the arguments
p.26 Autobiography	Continuous text, and photo
p.28 Persuasion	Poem with rhymes; last verse repeated from the first
p.30 Explanation	Website with headings in larger type, and photo
p.32 Report	Three sections of information
p.34 Instructions	Bullet points of magnifying glasses
p.36 Questionnaire	Q&A and photo
p.38 Leaflet	Picture map and text
p.40 Flier	Lots of different type styles, and illustration

Acknowledgements

Page 6: Fun poem — 'Lost rainbow' by Peter Dixon, reproduced in *Grow Your Own Poems* by Peter Dixon, 30 Cheriton Road, Winchester, Hants SO22 5AX, 1988, p. 9

Page 8: Poem to compare — 'The cracked ceiling' by Peter Dixon, reproduced in *Grow Your Own Poems* by Peter Dixon, 30 Cheriton Road, Winchester, Hants SO22 5AX, 1988, p. 12

Page 10: Riddle — 'Riddle 2', from *Rhymoceros* by Leo Aylen, p. 25

Page 16: History textbook — From *Black Settlers in Britain*, by Nigel File and Chris Power, Heinemann Educational Books, 1982. Reprinted with permission of Harcourt Education

Page 18: Historical novel — From *Abraham Hannibal and the Raiders of the Sands* by Frances Somers Cocks, Goldhawk Press, p. 168

Page 22: Fantasy novel: — From *The Ratastrophe Catastrophe* by David Lee Stone, Hodder Children's Books, p. 108. Reproduced by Permission of Hodder and Stoughton Limited

Page 24: Discussion — *Booktrusted News*, Book House, 45 East Hill, London SW18 2QZ. Extract from Terry Deary, 'Boys don't read', Issue 1, pp. 10–11, © Booktrusted News. For more information on children's books, please visit www.booktrusted.com

Page 26: Autobiography — *Booktrusted News*, Book House, 45 East Hill, London SW18 2QZ. Extract from 'Desert Island Books' Issue 1, p. 17, © Ian McMillan. Photograph of Ian McMillan by Simon Thackray

Page 28: Persuasion — RSPB, The Lodge, Sandy, Beds SG19 2DL. From *Bird Life*, May–June 2006, p. 11. Extract from 'The Albatross' © Ian McMillan

Page 30: Explanation — RSPB website © RSPB, www.savethe albatross.net

Page 32: Report — RSPB. From 'Well spotted', *Bird Life*, May–June 2006, p. 11. Artwork by Chris Shields, Andy Hamilton and Remy Ware; photographs by David Norton, rspb-images.com

Page 34: Instructions — RSPB. From 'Explore nature with a magnifying glass', *Bird Life*, May–June 2006, p. 23. Artwork by Mike Spoor, Bright Agency

Page 36: Questionnaire — RSPB. From 'Nice to meet you', *Bird Life*, May–June 2006, p. 5

Page 38: Leaflet — Leaflet of Barleylands Farm, Barleylands Road, Essex CM11, 2UD, info@barleylands.co.uk

Page 40: Flier — Artwork from 'The Wolves in the Walls'. Illustration by Dave McKean